DC SUPER HEROES

THE SCIENCE BEHIND SUPERMAN'S™ FLIGHT

Tammy Enz

Superman created by
Jerry Siegel and Joe Shuster
by special arrangement with
the Jerry Siegel family

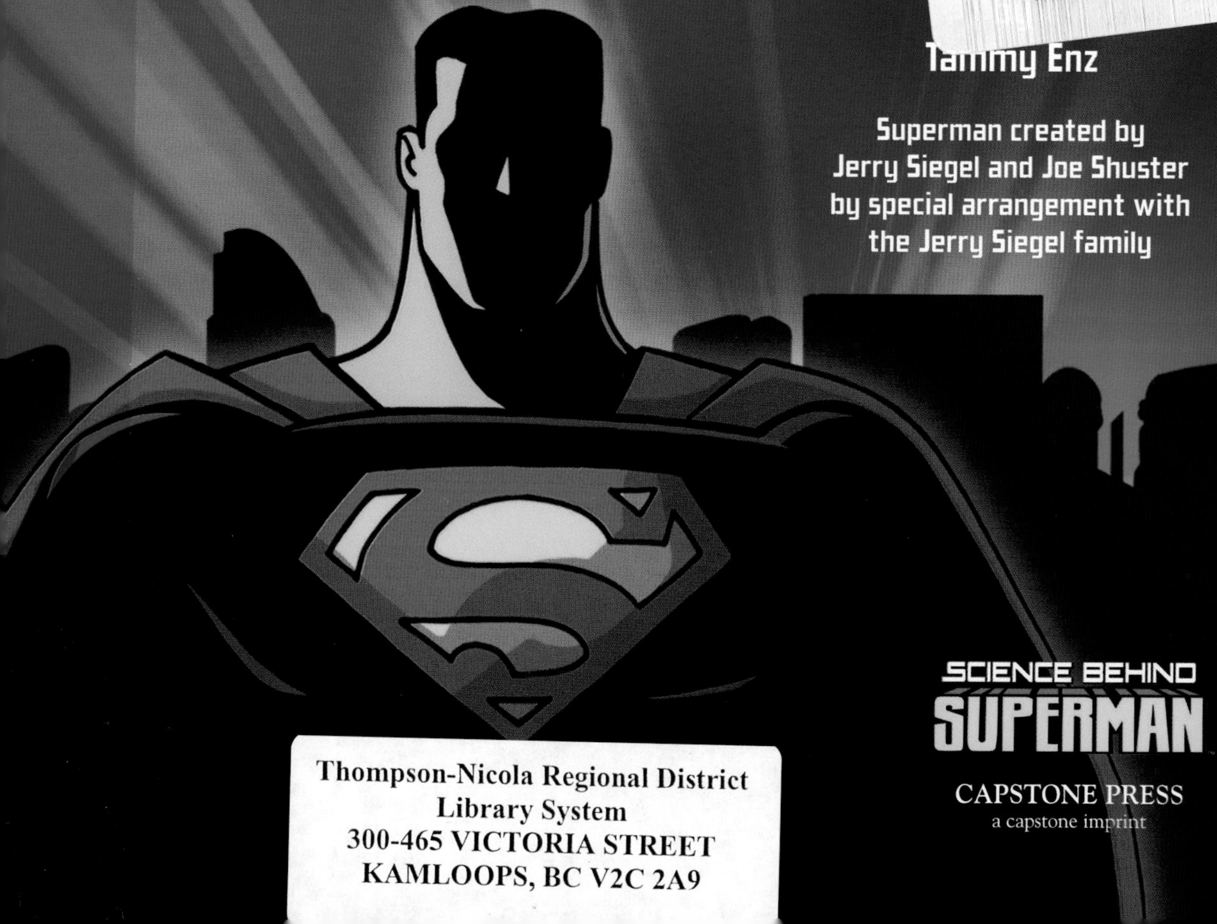

SCIENCE BEHIND SUPERMAN

CAPSTONE PRESS
a capstone imprint

Published by Capstone Press in 2017
A Capstone Imprint
1710 Roe Crest Drive
North Mankato, Minnesota 56003
www.mycapstone.com

STAR38177

Library of Congress Cataloging-in-Publication Data
Names: Enz, Tammy, author.
Title: The science behind Superman's flight / by Tammy Enz.
Description: North Mankato, Minnesota : Capstone Press, 2016. | Series: DC super heroes.
   Science behind Superman | Audience: Ages 7-9. | Audience: K to grade 3. | Includes bibliographical
   references and index.
Identifiers: LCCN 2016033216 (print) | LCCN 2016040872 (ebook) | ISBN 9781515750970 (library binding) |
   ISBN 9781515751014 (paperback) | ISBN 9781515751137 (eBook PDF)
Subjects: LCSH: Flight—Juvenile literature. | Aerodynamics—Juvenile literature. | Superman
   (Fictitious character)—Juvenile literature.
Classification: LCC TL547 .E58 2016 (print) | LCC TL547 (ebook) | DDC 629.132—dc23
LC record available at https://lccn.loc.gov/2016033216

Summary
Explores the science behind Superman's ability to fly and describes examples of flight from the real world.

Editorial Credits
Aaron Sautter, editor; Veronica Scott, designer; Kelly Garvin, media researcher;
Katy LaVigne, production specialist

Photo Credits
Capstone Press: Erik Doescher, backcover, 1, 3, 11, 14, 21, Luciano Vecchio, cover, 5, 9 (top), 17, 18, Min Sung
Ku, 22, Steve Mead, 8; Shutterstock: Celso Diniz, 20, Everett Historical, 9 (bottom inset), Keith Tarrier, 19, Natali
Glado, 10, Photobank gallery, 7, Radoslaw Lecyk, 12, Sindre T, 13, Steve byland, 15, Tony Campbell, 16; Warner
Brothers, 6

Printed and bound in the USA.
010023S17

Table of Contents

SOARING LIKE SUPERMAN

Superman has no wings. No engine. No special gear. But with a single leap, he can defy **gravity** and fly into the air. Humans don't have Superman's powers. But the science of flight lets people soar through the air in amazing ways.

FACT

Superman first appeared in comics in 1938. But at first he only leaped over tall buildings. He didn't begin flying until the early 1940s.

gravity—a force that pulls objects together; gravity pulls objects down toward the center of Earth

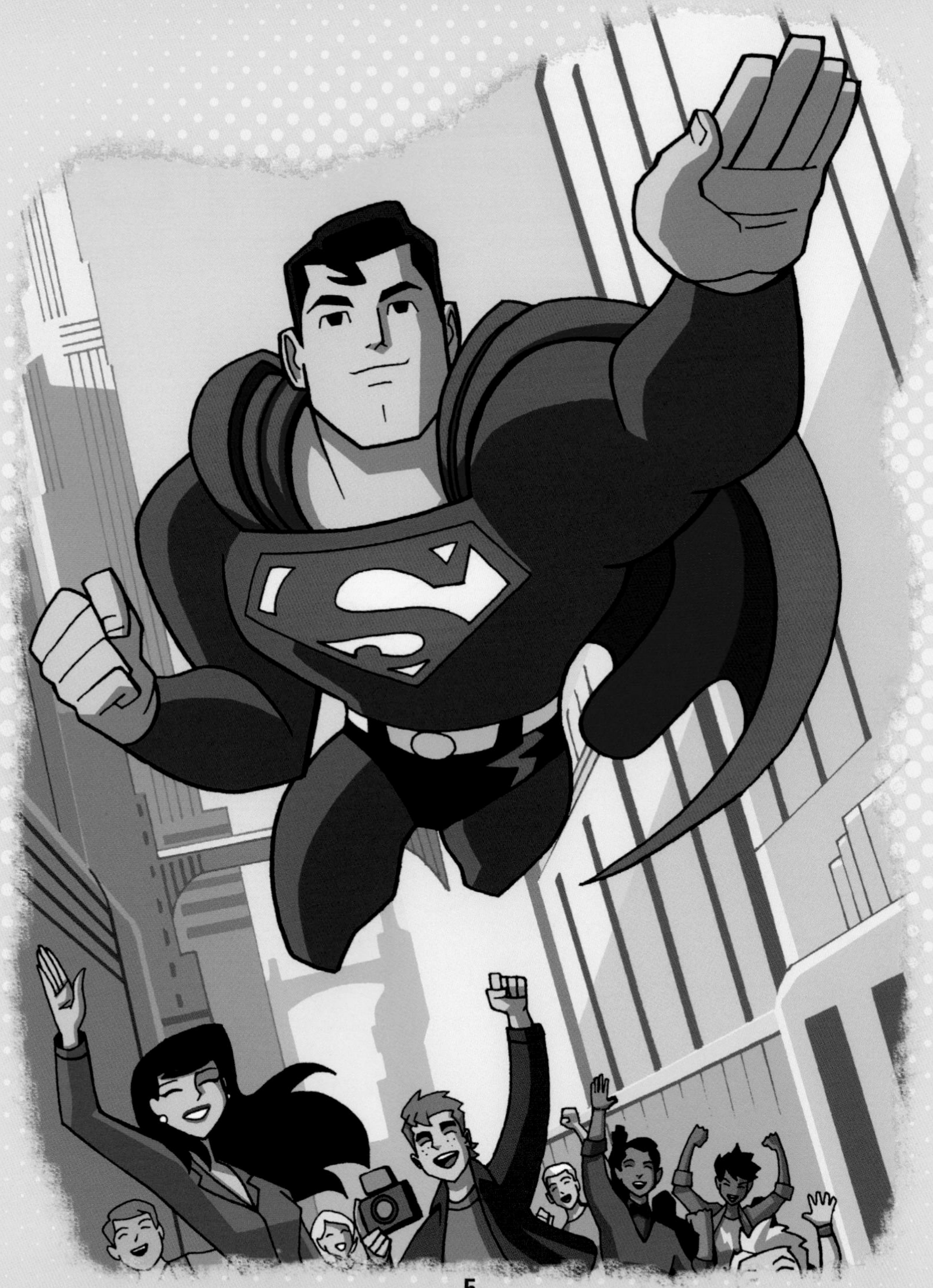

CHAPTER 1

FLYING INTO THE SKY

Flying comes naturally for Superman. But humans need the help of science to fly. An aircraft's powerful engines provide **thrust** to push it forward. Its wings are designed to create **lift**. This upward force helps the aircraft overcome gravity.

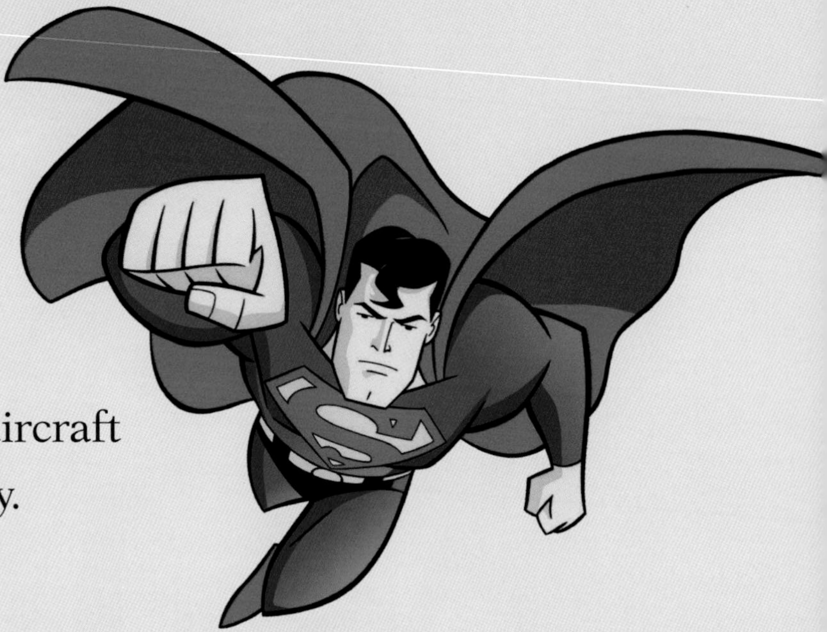

thrust—the force that pushes a vehicle forward

lift—the upward force that causes an object to rise into the air

FACT

Birds also use lift and thrust to fly. Their wings and feathers are shaped to help lift them into the air. They gain thrust by flapping their wings.

The curved shape of an airplane's wings creates lift. Air moves quickly over the top of the wings to create low **air pressure**. Meanwhile, air is pushed under the wings to create higher pressure. This higher pressure pushes up on the wings to create lift and raise the plane off the ground.

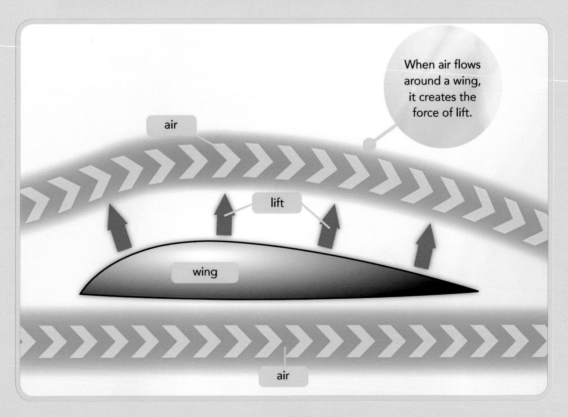

When air flows around a wing, it creates the force of lift.

air

lift

wing

air

air pressure—the force of air pushing against something

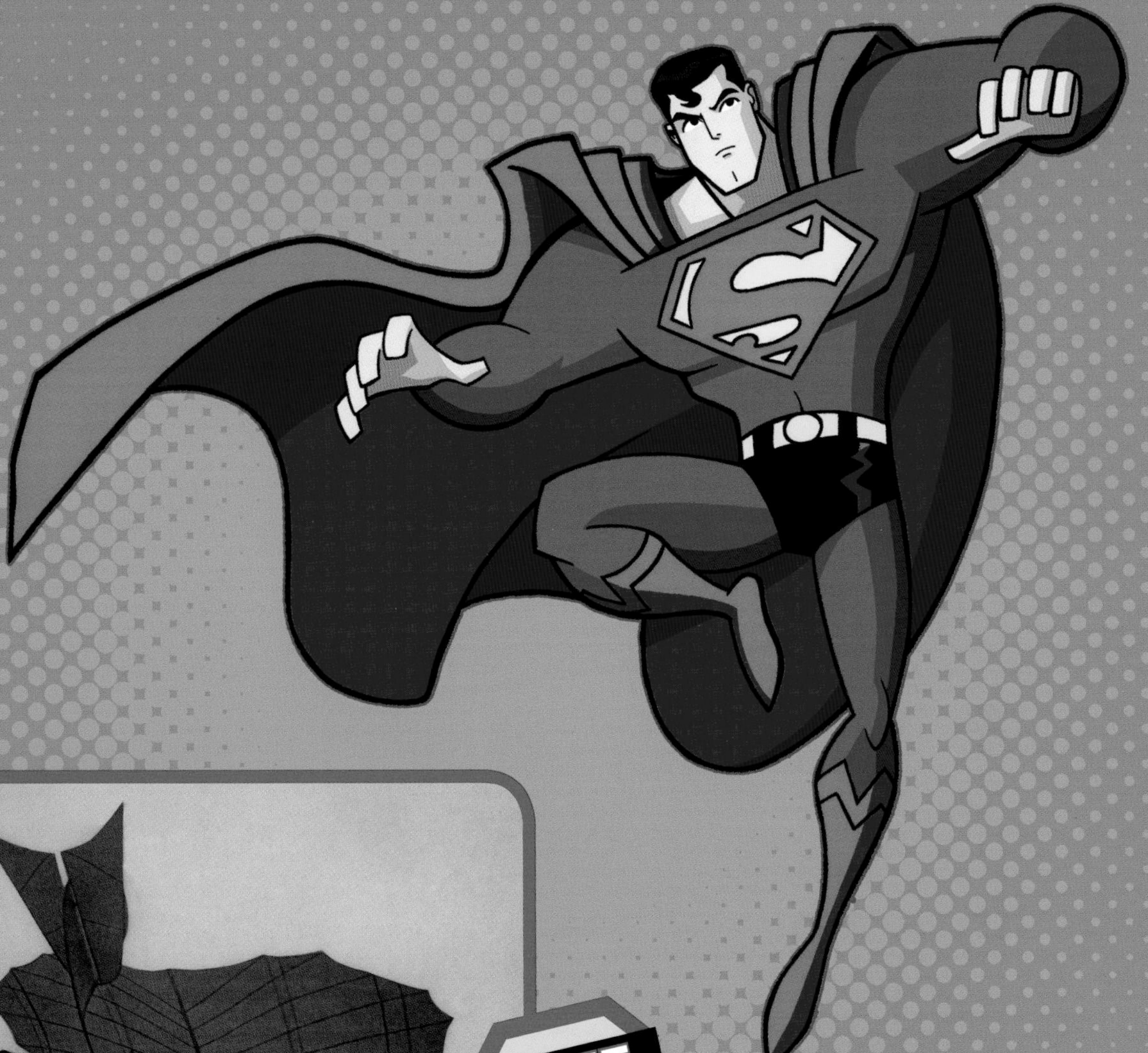

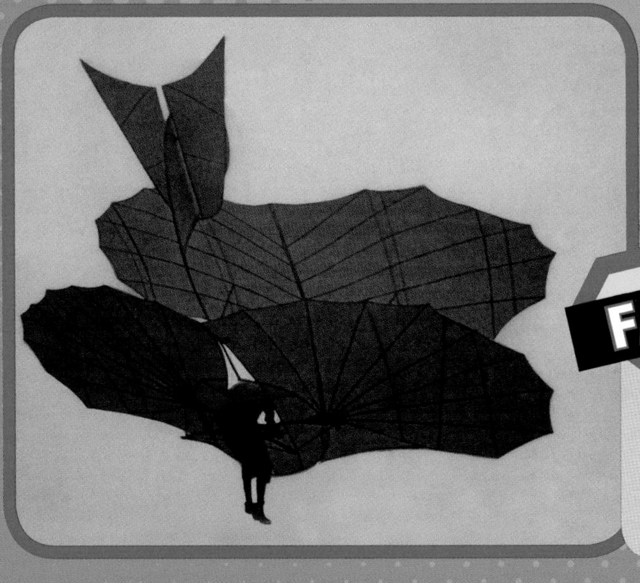

FACT

Otto Lilienthal created the first modern airplane wing design in the 1890s.

Helicopters use spinning **rotors** instead of wings to create lift. The rotors are shaped like an airplane's wings. As they spin, air flows over them to create high and low pressure. This action creates lift, which pushes the helicopter into the air. A tail rotor helps control the helicopter and keeps it stable.

rotor—a set of rotating blades that lifts an aircraft off the ground

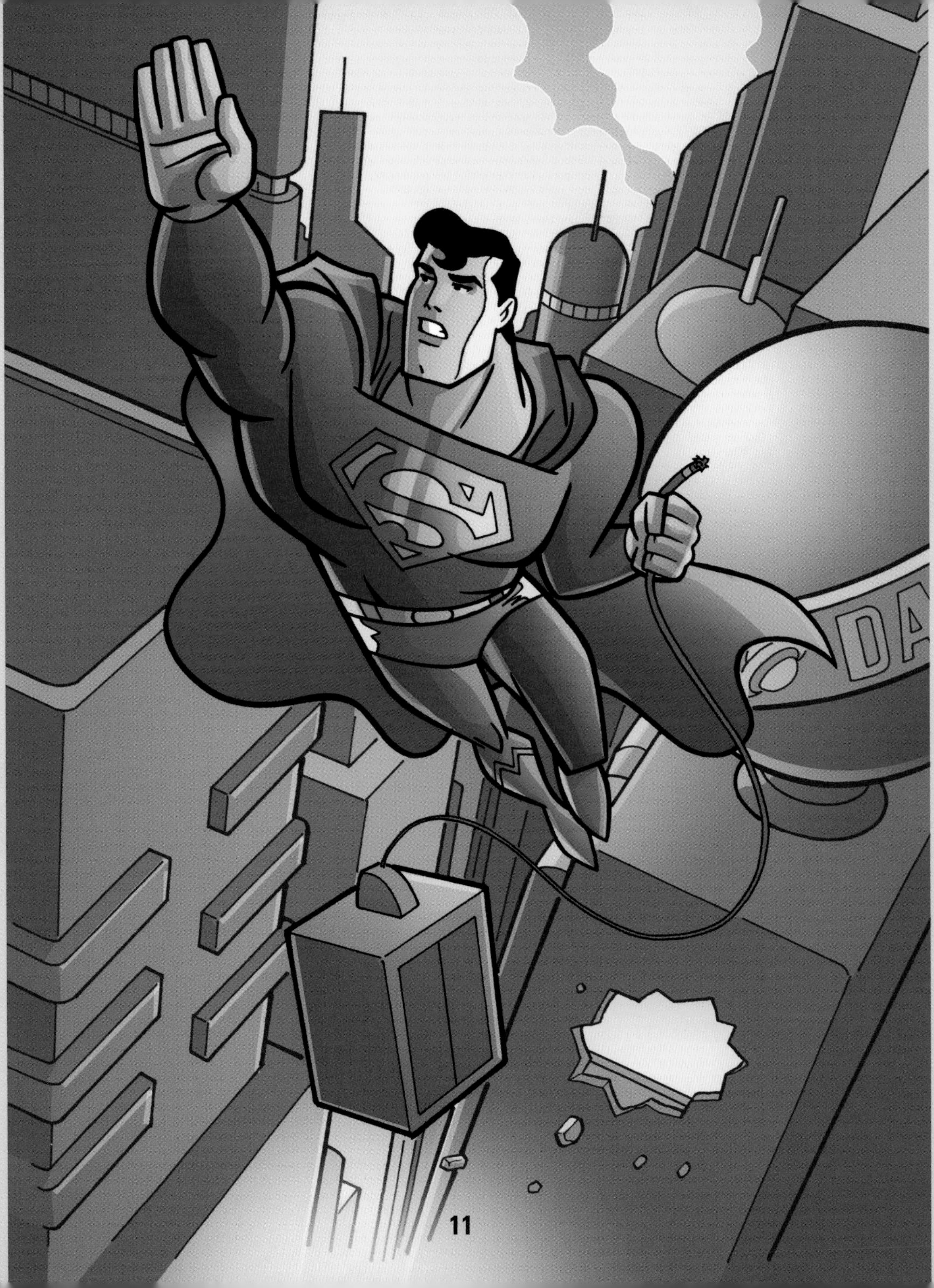
DA

Superman doesn't need wings or an engine to fly. People can also fly without them. Hang gliders and glider airplanes use **thermal lifts** to gain **altitude**. These aircraft can stay in the air for hours at a time. They can soar for hundreds of miles.

FACT

Wingsuits have arm and leg flaps to catch air after people jump from an airplane. Using wingsuits, people can soar through the air just like Superman. They use parachutes to land safely on the ground.

thermal lift—a rising pocket of warm air
altitude—the height of something above sea level or Earth's surface

CHAPTER 2

AMAZING ANIMAL FLYERS

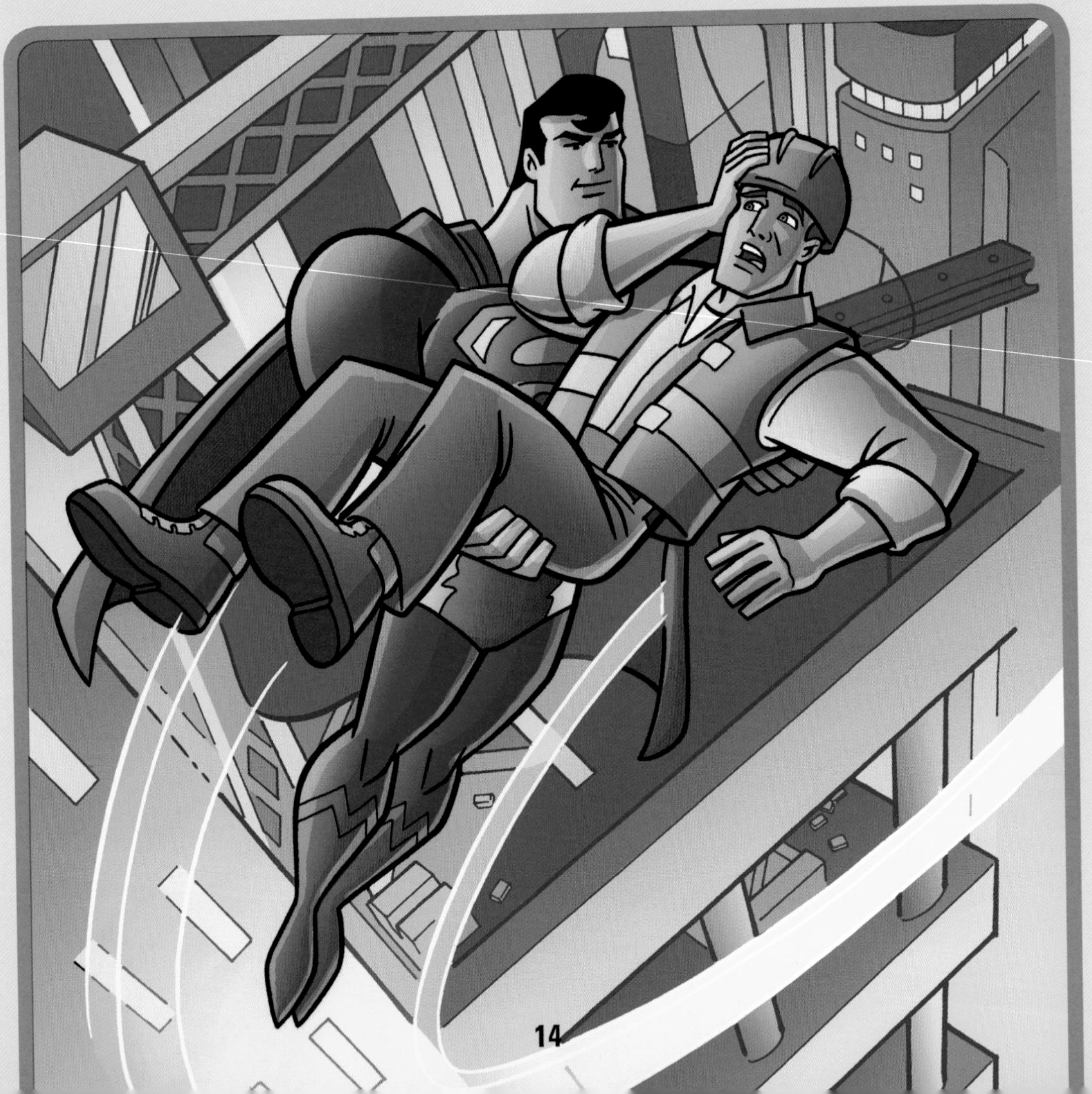

Superman isn't the only one to achieve incredible feats of flight. Around the world, many animals are also amazing flyers. Each year the Arctic tern **migrates** from Greenland to Antarctica. These birds fly up to 44,000 miles (71,000 kilometers) across the Atlantic ocean!

FACT

The ruby-throated hummingbird beats its wings 53 times each second. It can even fly upside down and backward!

migrate—to travel from one location to another

Birds aren't alone in the sky. Some squirrels and frogs can soar between the trees. How? Flying squirrels spread open the skin flaps between their legs. Wallace's flying frogs have **membranes** between their toes. They use these to help them glide from tree to tree.

flying squirrel

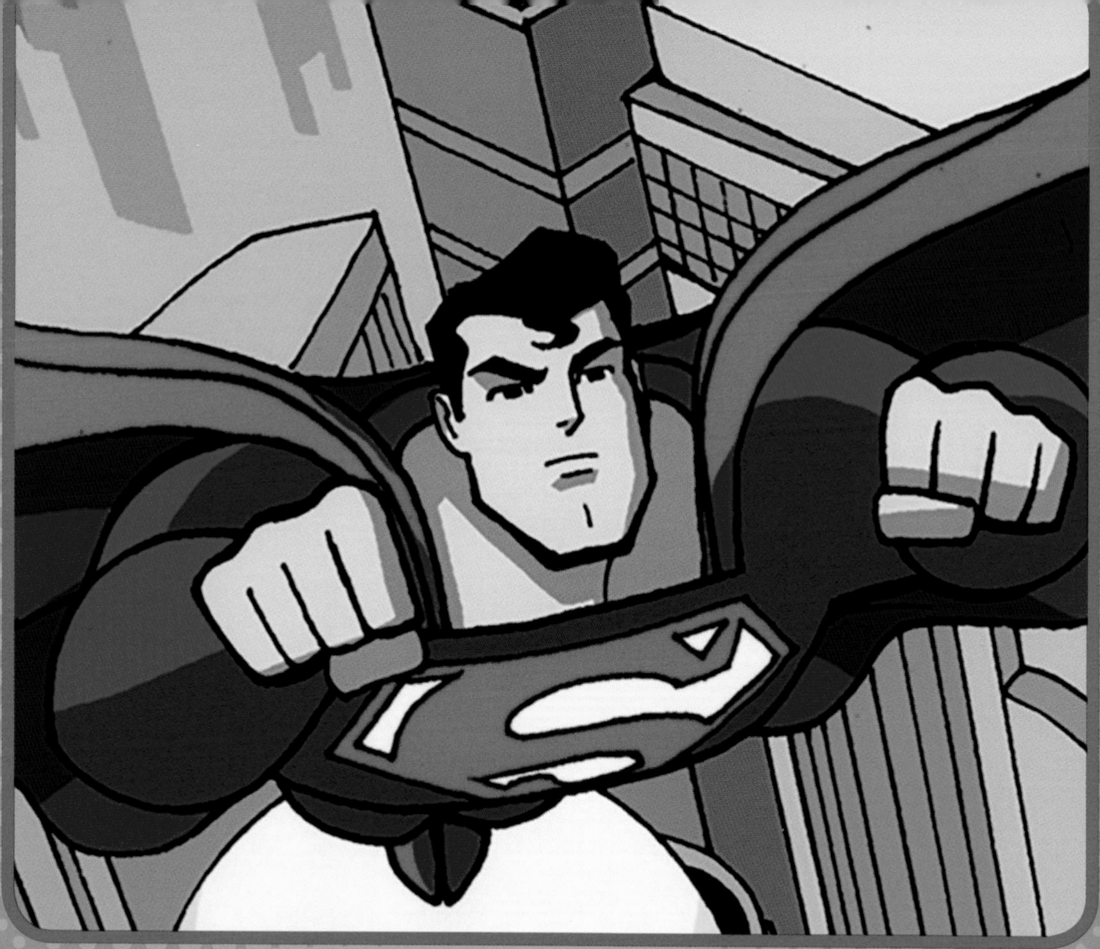

FACT

Flying fish rapidly beat their tails to launch from the sea. Then they glide above the water for up to 655 feet (200 meters) at a time!

membrane—a thin, flexible layer of tissue or skin

CHAPTER 3

ADVANCED FLYING MACHINES

Superman inspires people to fly higher, faster, and quieter. The SR-71 Blackbird was one of the fastest planes ever built. It flew more than 2,000 miles (3,219 km) per hour. The B-2 Spirit stealth bomber is shaped like a boomerang. It's designed to be quiet and nearly invisible to enemy **radar**.

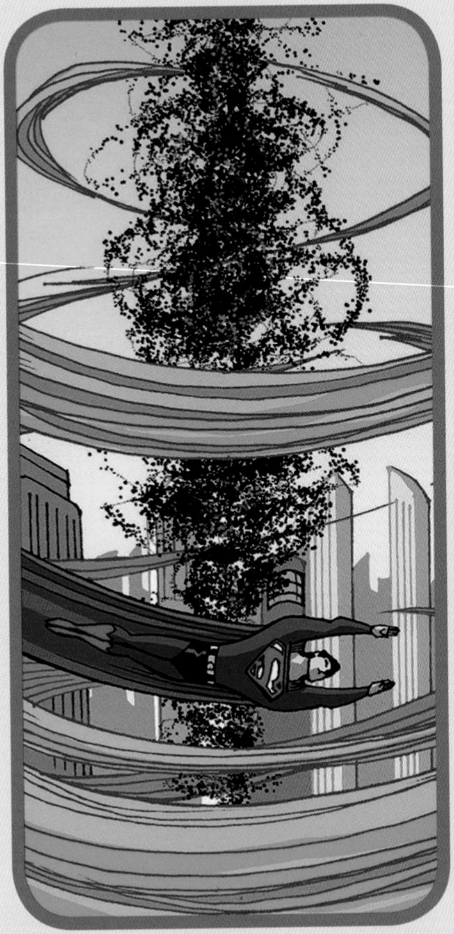

radar—a device that uses radio waves to track the location of objects

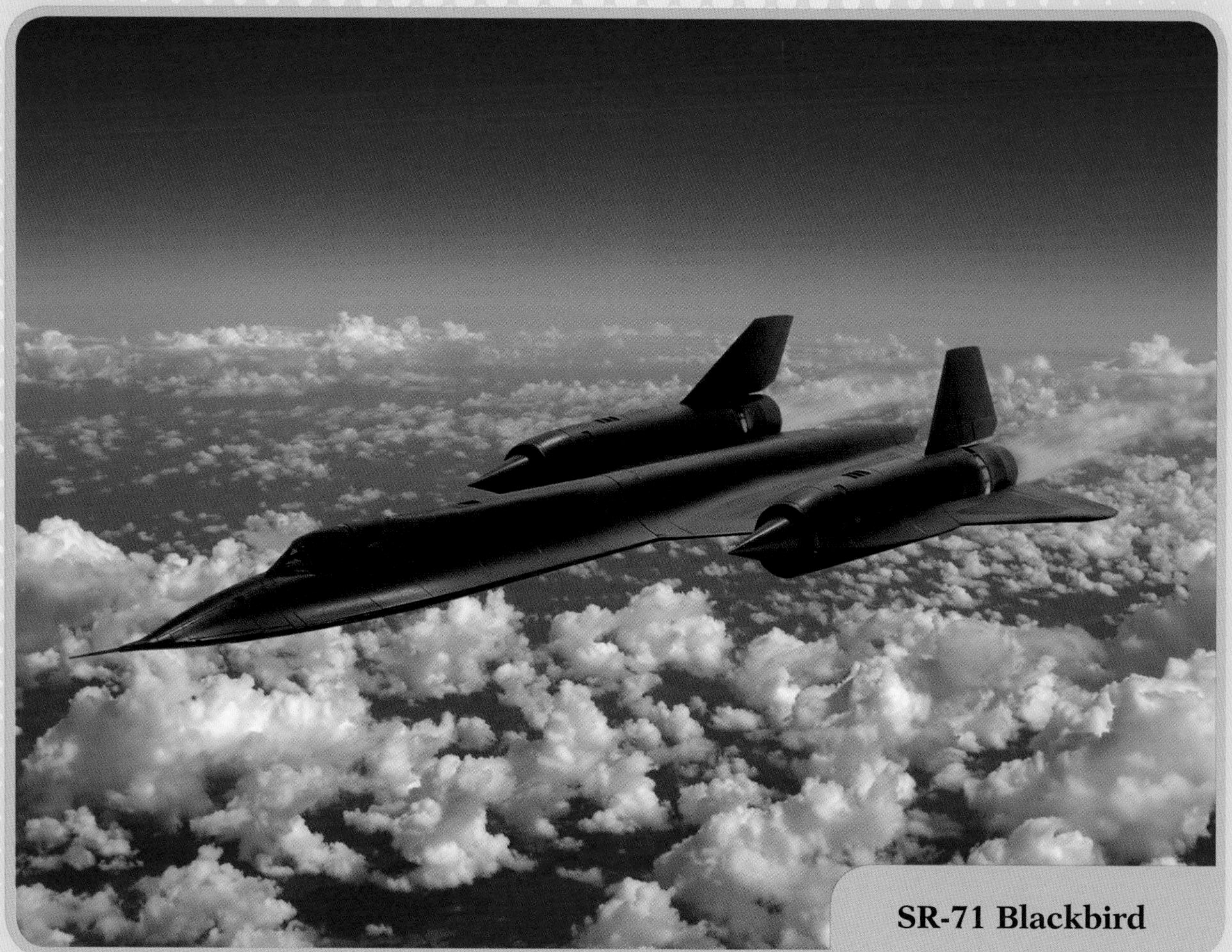

SR-71 Blackbird

Flying vehicles don't just soar through the air. Some fly into space. Rockets burn fuel to produce incredible thrust and escape Earth's gravity. Space vehicles have visited several planets in our solar system. Scientists hope to one day achieve **interstellar** flight and visit other stars.

interstellar—space between stars; often used to describe travel from one star to another

No human machine can compete with Superman. He can fly faster and farther than anyone can imagine. But from aircraft to spacecraft, science gives us a taste of what it's like to soar like Superman.

GLOSSARY

air pressure (AYR PRESH-ur)—the force of air pushing against something

altitude (AL-ti-tood)—the height of something above sea level or Earth's surface

gravity (GRAV-uh-tee)—a force that pulls objects together; gravity pulls objects down toward the center of Earth

interstellar (in-tur-STEL-ur)—space between stars; often used to describe travel from one star to another

lift (LIFT)—the upward force that causes an object to rise into the air

membrane (MEM-brayn)—a thin, flexible layer of tissue or skin

migrate (MYE-grate)—to travel from one location to another

radar (RAY-dar)—a device that uses radio waves to track the location of objects

rotor (ROH-tur)—a set of rotating blades that lifts an aircraft off the ground

thermal lift (THUR-muhl LIFT)—a rising pocket of warm air

thrust (THRUHST)—the force that pushes a vehicle forward

READ MORE

Enz, Tammy. *The Science Behind Batman's Flying Machines*. Science Behind Batman. North Mankato, Minn.: Capstone Press, 2016.

Nagelhout, Ryan. *Drones*. Military Machines. New York: Gareth Stevens, 2013.Capstone Press, 2012.

Royston, Angela. *Animals that Fly*. Adapted to Survive. Chicago: Capstone Raintree, 2014.

INTERNET SITES

FactHound offers a safe, fun way to find Internet sites related to this book. All of the sites on FactHound have been researched by our staff.

Here's all you do:
Visit *www.facthound.com*
Type in this code: 9781515750970

INDEX

READ THEM ALL!

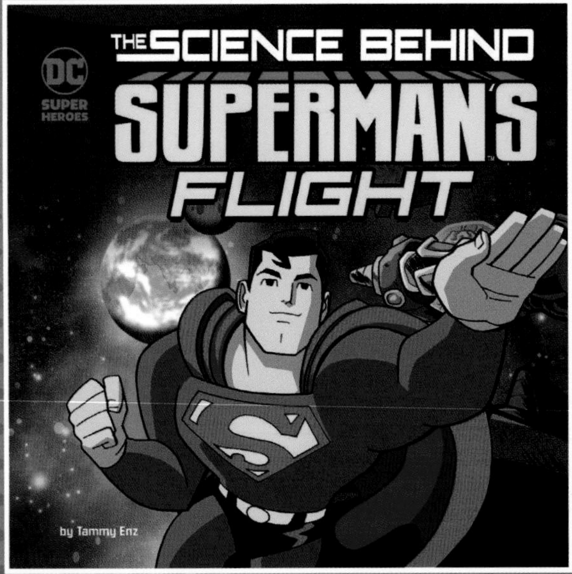
DC SUPER HEROES
THE SCIENCE BEHIND
SUPERMAN'S
FLIGHT
by Tammy Enz

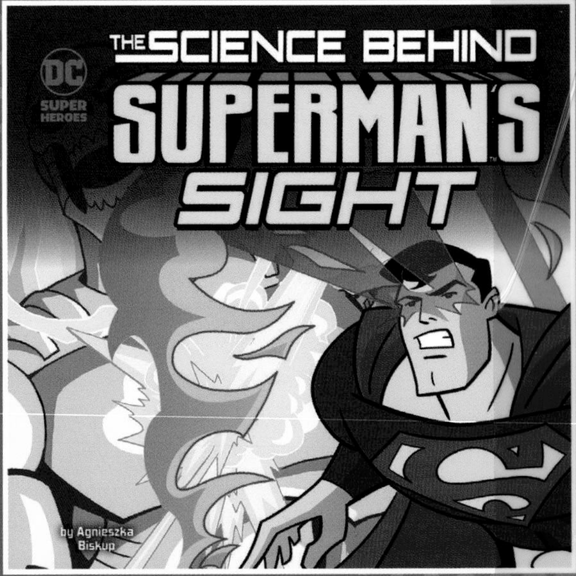
DC SUPER HEROES
THE SCIENCE BEHIND
SUPERMAN'S
SIGHT
by Agnieszka Biskup

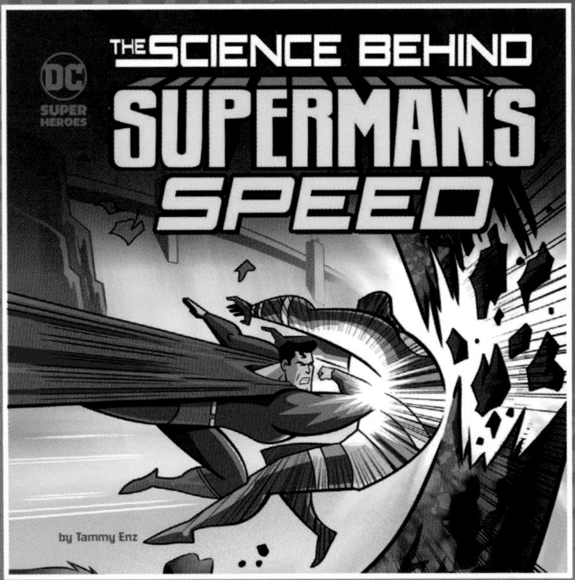
DC SUPER HEROES
THE SCIENCE BEHIND
SUPERMAN'S
SPEED
by Tammy Enz

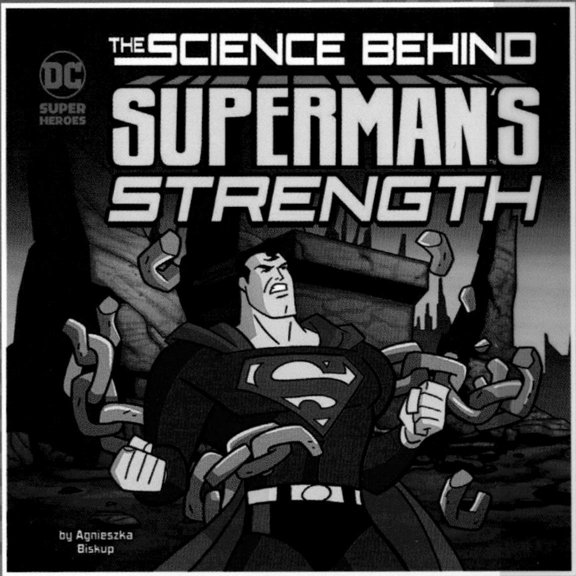
DC SUPER HEROES
THE SCIENCE BEHIND
SUPERMAN'S
STRENGTH
by Agnieszka Biskup